THE SALESPERSON'S POCKETBOOK

By Clive Bonny

Drawings by Phil Hailstone

"Full of practical advice which can be applied c~~~~
Mike Bennett, Sales Director, Nestlé

"Sensible suggestions for delivering straight.
Keith Stafford, Training Manager, Reuters

"Bite-size reminders to win new business and k~~~~~~~~~rs for life."
Gary Jennison, Sales Director, Barclays

Published by:
Management Pocketbooks Ltd
Laurel House, Station Approach, Alresford, Hants SO24 9JH, U.K.
Tel: +44 (0)1962 735573   Fax: +44 (0)1962 733637
E-mail: sales@pocketbook.co.uk
Website: www.pocketbook.co.uk

British Library Cataloguing-in-Publication Data – A catalogue record for this book is available from the British Library.

First published by Management Pocketbooks Ltd: 1991, Second edition: 2002. Reprinted 2004.

© Clive Bonny 1991, 2002

ISBN 1 870471 92 X

Design, typesetting and graphics by **efex ltd.**   Printed in U.K.

CONTENTS

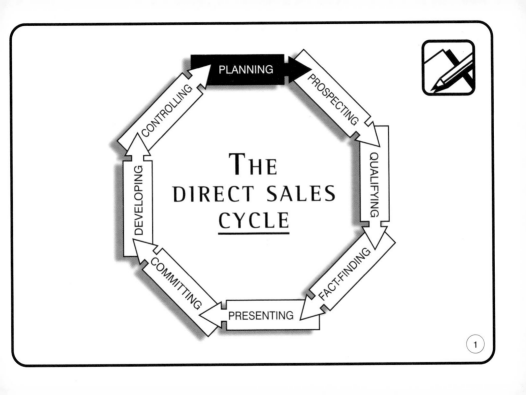

PLANNING

THE SALES PLAN

The first rule in preparing a sales plan is **KISS** – **K**eep **I**t **S**hort & **S**imple.

1.	**Summary**	Key results and activities, prioritised and timetabled
2.	**Background**	Marketplace profiles on customers, prospects and competitors
3.	**Targets**	Account names, potential (rate A-B-C) and schedule call plan
4.	**Methods**	Territory routes, timescales and special projects
5.	**Resource needs**	Equipment, support staff and training
6.	**Potential problems**	What if …
7.	**Contingencies**	… needs this action
8.	**Feedback**	Reporting channels and frequency
9.	**Costs and returns**	Forecast financial payback

Focus on your GOALS and customer needs

GOALS

TEN STEPS TO ACCOUNT DEVELOPMENT

Take one step at a time.

10. Build

9. Close

8. Propose

7. Fix buy criteria

6. Commit to change

5. Fact-find

4. Qualify want

3. List prospects

2. List suspects

1. Prioritise objectives

KEY RESULTS

GO FROM THE TOP DOWN

You are the foundation of organisational achievement.

Without **key results** you cannot judge good work.

NOR CAN ANYONE ELSE!

Core values

Company mission

Corporate strategy

Your manager's objectives

Your key results

Your key activities

TARGETS

SET MEATY TARGETS

Focus your planning with 'MEATY' targets.

M easurable

E ssential to the job

A chievable

T imetabled

Y our commitment

Examples
- Achieve quarterly forecast accuracy of at least 75%
- Clear all outstanding debts within 45 days
- Achieve minimum monthly revenue of 10,000
- Resolve all customer complaints in writing within one week
- Answer all incoming telephone calls within four rings

Don't bite off more than you can chew

PLANNING

KEY ACTIVITIES

Set 'MEATY' activity targets which are **essential** components of the key results.

Examples

- Report % likelihood of order status at month end
- Collect payment deposits with every order
- Submit at least 10 cost-justified proposals every month
- Reply to all complaints within two days of receipt
- Arrange continuous telephone manning 09.00 – 17.30 daily

If you don't know where or when you're going – you'll never arrive!

ATTITUDE

Your best resource is **yourself: ASK!**

A ttitude
S kill
K nowledge

It's half eaten   *There's half left*

ATTITUDE

Enthusiasm is the **cause** not **result** of **success**

Winners: **CAN DO**
                 WANT TO
                 WILL DO

Winners see the Point of Sale (**POS**):

P roblems as
O pportunities for
S olutions

SKILLS

RELATE AT ALL LEVELS

Personal qualities for success:

Essential

- Resilience
- Honesty
- Energy
- Strategic awareness
- Problem solving skills

Desirable

- Perseverance
- Sensitivity
- Initiative
- People skills
- Confidence

9

KNOWLEDGE

It is essential that you have knowledge of:

- Company mission
- Strategy
- Your manager's goals
- Your key results and activities
- Products and services
- Policies and procedures
- Support staff
- Customers' needs
- Other suppliers

PLANNING

KNOWLEDGE

If you can't remember it, **carry** it. Check your **briefcase tool kit**.

- Order forms
- Pricing
- Testimonials
- Brochures
- Calculator
- Service agreements
- Trading terms
- Planner diary

- Cost-benefit examples
- Business cards
- Survey checklist
- Key telephone numbers
- Competitor analysis
- Client records
- Blank paper

And keep it tidy!

BENEFITS

BE FAB

- Focus on **benefits** not features (make sure you know the difference)

Feature	**A**dvantage	**B**enefit
It is	It does	It does for you

eg: a bulb	gives light	for you to see

- Test with *So what's in it for them?*

BENEFIT STATEMENTS

REMEMBER YOUR P's & Q's

Prioritise: *How important is it?*
Quantify: *How much will it save?*

Develop benefit statements related to **their interests**.
Give them **'you'** appeal.

Appeal to:
- Personal **wants** – prestige, fear of loss
- Company **needs** – more profit, lower costs
- Their **job-related goals**

(13)

PLANNING

RESOURCES

Your manager
- Use his/her experience and knowledge
- Forewarn him/her of problems

Your team meetings
- Hold outside peak selling hours
- Plan agenda objectives
- Listen actively
- Don't interrupt
- Don't criticise without constructive comments
- Agree action, by whom, by when

RESOURCES

Team colleagues

- Swop your expertise for theirs
- Observe them on the job
- Invite them to coach you
- Praise them

Support staff

- Explain your objectives and understand theirs
- Don't set unrealistic deadlines
- Absorb their client knowledge
- Thank them

PARTNERING

PUT YOURSELF IN THEIR SHOES

Do clients see you as a **Protagonist** or **Partner**?

Partnership Sale Steps:

CLIENT		SALESPERSON		ACTION
Problem not identified		Identified		Joint Identification
Problem identified		Measured		Joint solution

PARTNERING

Your strategy should ensure a win-win result for both parties.

Tactics:
- Focus on **big** issues
- Offer quantified financial benefits
- Install controls to measure benefits
- Treat them as unique
- Talk their language
- Don't oversell
- Be a problem-solver; examine alternatives
- Keep contact with the top decision-maker

PARTNERING

Move from	To
Sell	Consult
Implement	Facilitate
React	Be proactive
Tell	Listen
Your solution	Their solution
Costs	Cost-benefits

PLANNING

TIME MANAGEMENT

- Work expands to fill the time available
  (Parkinson's Law)

- Set yourself deadlines
  for each task

19

TIME MANAGEMENT

Plan: Invest time to save time

- Assess time available; 20 working days per month
- Deduct time needed for travel, writing reports, etc, and actual selling time (10 days?)
- Allocate time needed for key activities, eg: phoning, visiting
- Record **actual** time spent on key activities
- Focus on discrepancies between **actual** and **target**
- Set improvement targets, eg: number of:
  - telephone calls per appointment
  - appointments per proposal
  - proposals per order

TIME MANAGEMENT

Have **A MAP**

A lways work on **key activities** first

M ake a **daily To Do** list

A ction   A   Important AND Urgent ('must')
              B   Important NOT Urgent ('should')
              C   Urgent not Important ('could')

P rioritise A – B – C order **daily**

TIME MANAGEMENT

- **In the car**
  - Carry key records
  - Use a dictaphone

- **In the office**
  - Handle mail once only
  - Batch together similar tasks

- **In meetings**
  - Time-frame agendas
  - Stick to schedule

- **In projects**
  - Break big jobs into small tasks
  - Build in contingency time

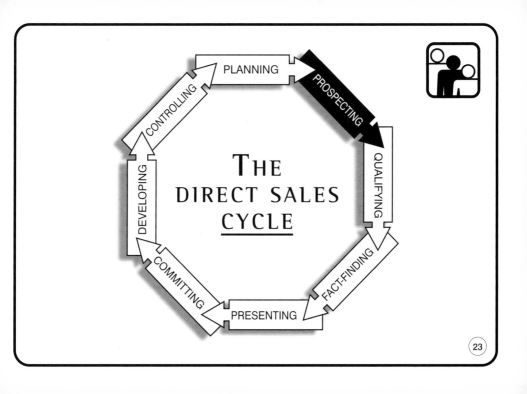

INFORMATION SOURCES

The following can be good sources of information for finding prospects:

- **Your office** - Sales leads, client records, colleagues, suppliers
- **Clients' offices** - Receptionists, their suppliers, newsletters, notices, contacts moving jobs, annual reports
- **Press** - Trade journals, local news, clippings services
- **Lists** - Exhibition attendees, industrial databases, electronic data services, credit raters
- **Others** - Trade and professional bodies, embassies, chambers of commerce, relatives, friends, internet

DIRECT MAIL
BROAD MAILSHOT

- Strategy: Identify prospects buying soon
- Tactics: Test run and monitor success percentage by source

Content

- Address by name, not *Sir/Madam*
- State main **benefit** to them
- Quote testimonial or proof
- Highlight key words
- Sign it

(25)

DIRECT MAIL

BROAD MAILSHOT

- **Limit to**
  - One page
  - Five lines per paragraph
  - 14 words per sentence

- **Use**
  - Letterhead paper
  - Centre layout
  - Short positive words
  - P.S. to prompt immediate action
  - Reply card or pre-addressed envelope

- **Avoid**
  - Unconditional *give-aways*

PROSPECTING

DIRECT MAIL

FOCUSED MAILSHOT

Goal
- Fix appointment with decision-maker

Strategy
- Arouse demand for more information

Tactics
- Check by phone decision-maker's name and title
- Use 'you' not 'I' in letter
- Put yourself in their shoes
- Sign it personally
- Do it outside peak selling time
- Don't include product details
- Follow-up by phone within a week

DIRECT MAIL
FOCUSED MAILSHOT

Use **A I D A** to structure your mailshot:

A ttention: Introduce with personalised **'you'** appeal

I nterest: Show **how** it affects them

D esire: Explain **benefits** to them

A ction: **Stimulate** their action/confirm your follow-up

APPOINTMENTS BY PHONE
AIM FOR THE CENTRE

Your target is to speak to the person
who decides.

D ecider: Authorises budget

R ecommender: Manages users

U ser: Implements and influences

G atekeeper: *Experts* and secretaries

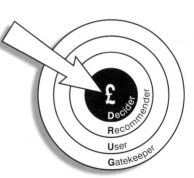

APPOINTMENTS BY PHONE

KEY STEPS IN THE CALL STRUCTURE

Thank
Fact-find
Fix appointment
Overcome objections
Ask for appointment
Qualify wants & needs
Stimulate interest
Establish rapport
Identify yourself

PROSPECTING

MAKING APPOINTMENTS

INTRODUCTION STATEMENTS

- **Switchboard**
  - Be warm: *Can you help me?*
  - Verify decision-maker's name, title and address

- **Secretary**
  - Control with questions
  - *It concerns policy regarding X. Is she/he in?*
  - *Do you keep his/her diary or should I call back later?*
  - *What time would be best?*

- **P.A. to M.D.**
  - *Would you know who decides policy on X?*
    (then transfer directly …)
  - *… Miss Jones suggested I spoke with you*

- **Decision-maker**
  - Give full name and check they're not in a meeting
  - Use a **hook**: *I read that you have recently …*
  - Match your benefit statement to their job function

MAKING APPOINTMENTS

Before the call
- Prepare
  - Activity goals for the day
  - Opening benefit statements
  - Likely objections and replies
  - Best times and places for you

During the call
- Qualify
  - **W** ants
  - **A** uthority
  - **N** eeds
  - **T** imescale
  - **S** pending power

After the call
- Replace phone on hook last
- Confirm in writing: date, time, place, purpose

MAKING APPOINTMENTS

Do

- ✔ Make notes
- ✔ Be persistent
- ✔ Sound confident
- ✔ Ask for appointments at 08.45, 11.45, 13.45, 16.15 hours
- ✔ Offer alternative times, one specific and one open:
  - *Are you free 08.45 am Friday …*
  - *… or is some time next week more convenient?*

Don't

- ✘ Wait on hold
- ✘ Accept *We'll call you back*
- ✘ Pause between benefit statement and question
- ✘ Talk to purchasing departments

SELLING BY PHONE

- Follow structure as for appointments (page 30).

- Build testimonials into benefit statements: *Your manufacturers were delighted with us. I'd like to show why.*

- Test close: *How does that sound?*

- Close direct: *Can we go ahead?*
  - alternative offer: *Can we deliver this month or next?*
  - minor offer: *Can we deliver the extras the same day?*
  - assumed offer: *To whom shall we address the invoice?*

- Ring **ENTHUS**
  - **I**
  - **A**m
  - **S**old
  - **M**yself

WORD PICTURES

Use positive, active language to create the right atmosphere.

Avoid	**Use**
Negative/Passive	Positive/Active
(eg: *It could be arranged*)	(eg: *We can arrange*)

Avoid	Use
Pay	Invest
Suggest	Recommend
Change	Improve
Sign	Approve
If	When
I	You

BUILDING RAPPORT

In advance: Avoid distractions, smile, relax

During: Make notes, check back

Match their personalities (see pages 46-49):

	Words with	Tone	Example
INSPIRER	emotions	enthusiastic	*vital, great*
ASPIRER	goals	direct/concise	*progress, decide*
ENQUIRER	facts	logical/slow	*data indicates*
ADMIRER	empathy	warm/open	*believe, understand*

OBJECTION HANDLING
POSE 'SUPPOSE'

Reply to possible objections with 'suppose' statements. Examples:

- No budget:
  Suppose it paid for itself, you'd be interested, wouldn't you?
- Too busy:
  Suppose we fixed a time next month when we're both free?
- Send me literature:
  Suppose we saved you 30 minutes' reading time instead.
- No need to change suppliers:
  Suppose we gave you better value …

 Then ask for an appointment **without pausing**.

PROSPECTING

CHECKLIST

Checklist to use before making new appointments:

1. Have up-to-date information on their strategic market forces
2. Use network contacts for current grapevine news
3. Read their latest company report and literature
4. Draft benefit statements linked to their strategy
5. Check top PA's name and title at reception
6. Ask for the top PA's help
7. Qualify when key people are accessible
8. Check they are not in a meeting
9. Give them ways to say yes

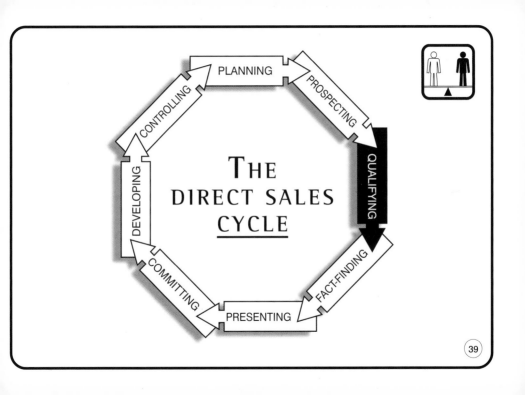

THE
DIRECT SALES
CYCLE

PLANNING
PROSPECTING
QUALIFYING
FACT-FINDING
PRESENTING
COMMITTING
DEVELOPING
CONTROLLING

INCOMING TELEPHONE CALLS

- Have a message pad at hand
- Pick up within four rings
- Write down caller's name, company, number
- Ask source:
  - *How did you hear of us?*
  - *What prompted your enquiry?*
  - *Who else is involved in approving this?*
  - *What are you looking for?*
  - *When would you like to install?*
  - *How much are you intending to invest?*
- Qualify
  - **W** ants
  - **A** uthority
  - **N** eeds
  - **T** imescale
  - **S** pending power

INCOMING SALES CALLS

- Sell across range:
  Our clients are taking advantage of our special offer …

- Sell up range:
  Did you know that if you took brand X then you could …

- Sell your uniqueness:
  *We're the only company who supply U.S.B.s for **your** needs*

Unique **S**ales **B**enefits

FIRST VISITS

You get only **one chance** to make a first impression.

Preparation in reception:

- Ensure a positive attitude
- Rehearse call objectives
- Check for evidence of competitors
- Read client literature

Introduction:

- Smile
- Ask about a personal interest
- Ask permission to take notes
- Note names, roles, objectives, time available
- Agree next steps

FIRST VISITS

Qualify **WANTS**:
- **W** ants – exactly what are they looking for
- **A** uthorities: decision-making process
- **N** eeds of their personal and organisational goals
- **T** imescale of their evaluation and implementation
- **S** pend capacity, whose budget and when available

Probe:
- Knowledge of applications and competitors
  - *How much research has been undertaken so far?*
- Next process stage
  - *What is the next step?*
- Previous buying pattern and experience
  - *What improvements would you like to see?*
- The operational and cost impact of **not** improving

DECISION PROCESS

IDENTIFY THOSE INVOLVED

You need to identify all those involved in the decision-making chain.

- Distinguish:

➤ Role $\Rightarrow$ **Purpose** of job

➤ Responsibility $\Rightarrow$ **Main function** of job-holder

➤ Authority level $\Rightarrow$ **Sign-off limits**

- Define if *active* or *passive* role
  Active = **improver** of status quo
  Passive = **keeper** of status quo

- Check any committee involved in the decision:
  chairperson, agenda, meeting dates, to whom it reports

AUTHORITIES

CATEGORISE THE CHAIN OF COMMAND

When making contact, work from the highest level downwards, from Authority to User.
Then return to Authority and Recommender together.

1 **Authority**   Authorises and signs off

2 **Recommender**   Approves

3 **Influencer**   Offers specialist advice
   (Make their job easy!)

4 **User**   Hands-on implementer

5 **Gatekeeper**   Filters out supplier contact
   (Avoid them!)

PERSONALITY TYPES
INSPIRER

- Driven by   people, own prestige, company mission
- High on   interaction, expression, intuition, assertion
- Low on   caution, detail, facts, figures
- Wants   acclaim
- Appeal to   self-image, quality, innovation
- Method   listen, enthuse, say *Who*
- Office   personal symbols and pictures, chairs close and different
- Hands   in front

PERSONALITY TYPES
ASPIRER

- Driven by goals, own objectives, company effectiveness
- High on assertion, control, direction, pressure
- Low on caution, detail, expression, time
- Wants results
- Appeal to productivity, personal gain
- Method cost-benefits, options, say *What*
- Office achievement symbols, chairs apart and different
- Hands behind head

47

PERSONALITY TYPES

ENQUIRER

- Driven by   goals, own recognition, company efficiency
- High on   caution, planning, facts, logic, time
- Low on   expression, assertion, interaction
- Wants   justification
- Appeal to   cost-saving, curiosity
- Method   market research, comparisons, say *Why*
- Office   graphs, neat paperwork, chairs apart and similar
- Hands   on chin

48

PERSONALITY TYPES

ADMIRER

- Driven by   people, own recognition, company standards
- High on   caution, listening, rapport, time
- Low on   assertion, control, pressure, change
- Wants   security
- Appeal to   reliability, low risk
- Method   market trends, testimonials, say *How*
- Office   people pictures, untidy papers, chairs close and similar
- Hands   over mouth

49

PERSONALITY TYPES

SUMMARY

INSPIRERS	prefer to talk and to enthuse **Recognise their successes and their visions**
ASPIRERS	prefer directness and efficiency **Stress opportunities and fast results**
ENQUIRERS	prefer options with supportive detail **Give a logical approach and time to think**
ADMIRERS	prefer solutions with proof statements **Supply testimonials from satisfied clients**

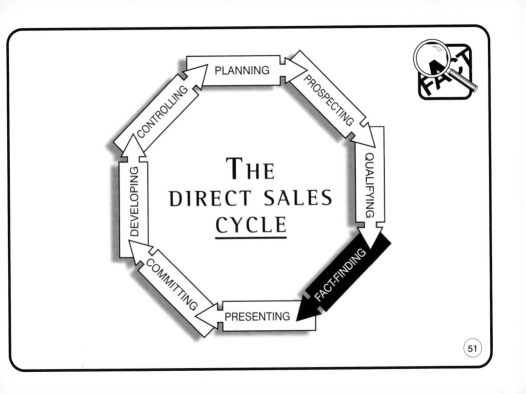

THE
DIRECT SALES
CYCLE

PLANNING
PROSPECTING
QUALIFYING
FACTFINDING
PRESENTING
COMMITTING
DEVELOPING
CONTROLLING

FACT

51

NEEDS ANALYSIS

DOCTOR'S APPROACH

- Talk to the head

- Note history and symptoms

- Check the body

- Diagnose problem

- Consider best solution

- Discuss and agree treatment

HANDY QUESTIONS

- Arouse **attention**

- Make people **think**

- Help **absorb** key points

- Clarify **progress**

- Increase **self-confidence**

- Create **commitment and partnership**

KEEPING CONTROL

- Control the speed and **PACE** of the discussion

P rovide information
A ssess non-verbal signals
C larify progress
E xplore feelings

- Use open questions to probe, eg: *Who, Why, What, When, How?*

- Use **closed** questions (eg: answer *Yes* or *No*) to **re-direct** or **summarise**, eg: *Are you saying that …?*

QUESTIONS

GO ON A SPREE

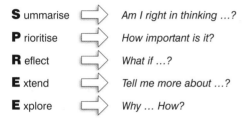

S ummarise ⟹ *Am I right in thinking …?*

P rioritise ⟹ *How important is it?*

R eflect ⟹ *What if …?*

E xtend ⟹ *Tell me more about …?*

E xplore ⟹ *Why … How?*

- Avoid **ego**
  Not *I think* but *What do you think?*

- If **sensitive** area, ask if you can ask:
  Would you mind me asking what you think of …?

- Express it **positively**:
  Not *Tell me about your problems* but *Which areas would you like to improve?*

FACT-FINDING

KEY QUESTIONS

W ants	• *What would you like to improve most?*
	• *What is the impact of no improvement?*
	• *What alternatives are being considered?*
A uthority	• *Who else is involved in evaluating and approving?*
N eeds	• *What are your key goals?*
	• *What issues stand in the way?*
T imescale	• *When will you complete evaluation and installation?*
S pend	• *How much money has been allocated?*
	• *Which budget will it come from?*

RESPONSES TO QUESTIONS

When they reply to your questions:

✔ Pause

✔ Check back   ⟹   *What do you mean by ...?*

✔ Prioritise   ⟹   *How big an issue is it?*

✔ Build up   ⟹   *So if you couldn't do that then ...?*

✔ Clarify   ⟹   *So what you mean is ...?*

✔ Understand their issue as real and unique

✘ Don't **GAG**: **G** ive unsolicited advice

                A ssume

                G eneralise

57

FACT-FINDING

ACTIVE LISTENING
WHY NOBODY'S HEARD OF IT

	Listen	Speak	Read	Write
Order learned	1	2	3	4
Used	45%	30%	16%	9%
Taught	Least	Next least	Next most	Most

ACTIVE LISTENING

Our 500 most used words have over 10,000 dictionary definitions.

- One word 'set' has: 126 verbal uses
  + 58 noun uses
  + 10 adjective uses

- Listen to **how** words are **SPEC**ified:
  S peed
  P ronunciation
  E mphasis
  C ontext

ACTIVE LISTENING

Do:
- ✔ Watch their eyes
- ✔ Suppress your feelings
- ✔ Check understanding
- ✔ Use notes

Don't:
- ✗ Be distracted
- ✗ Interrupt
- ✗ Miss implied needs
- ✗ Queue up your next question

FACT-FINDING

FEASIBILITY SURVEY

Offer to conduct a feasibility survey to establish the potential benefits to the client of your proposal.

Process

- Gain acceptance of need to survey requirements
- Justify why now
- Fix top-down contact route
- Issue advance agenda
- Interview individually
- Emphasise your interest in **their** personal goals
- Help them to identify issues:
    - **operational impact** on themselves
    - **costs** of issues
    - **cost-benefits** to themselves

KEY COST-BENEFITS

Look for cost-benefits in the following areas:

HIGHER

- Working capital
- Productivity
- Revenue
- Profit

LOWER

- Costs
- Aged debt
- Staff attrition

COST-BENEFIT ANALYSIS

 Calculate benefits in **time and productivity** and convert into **money**

Build **cost-savings** into their **cost centres**

Build **earnings** into their **profit centres**

Minimise your **costs** with **finance** options

Maximise return with **long-term** projection

CHECKLIST

Checklist when meeting prospective clients:

1. Analyse and adapt to their personal style
2. Emphasise your role to support their goals
3. Ask permission to take notes
4. Ask about their organisation strategies
5. Ask about their personal priorities
6. Ask them to expand on the *ripple effect* of issues
7. Ask them to estimate impact on cost and revenue
8. Counter-balance their costs with your cost-benefits
9. Build your uniqueness into their purchasing criteria
10. Reinforce with case studies and proof statements

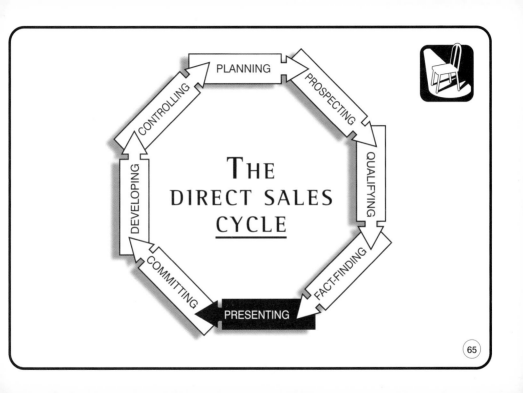

THE
DIRECT SALES
CYCLE

PLANNING
PROSPECTING
QUALIFYING
FACT-FINDING
PRESENTING
COMMITTING
DEVELOPING
CONTROLLING

65

PREPARATION

1. **Prepare**
- Why? ⇨ Purpose
- Who? ⇨ Audience
- When? ⇨ Timing
- What? ⇨ Content
- How? ⇨ Delivery
- Which? ⇨ Tools

2. **Rehearse**
3. **Ask for feedback**

PRESENTING

TOOLS

VISUAL DISPLAY

Lettering should be:
BOLD **B**LOCK **C**ONSISTENT
Max 8 lines of 8 words
Max 30 numerals

Symbols

Charts

Cartoons

Pointers

Don't
✗ Have numbers in columns or use a kaleidoscope of colours

Do
✔ Talk-write-talk and flip when finished

TOOLS

POWERPOINT

If preparing a Powerpoint presentation:

- **C**heck system compatibility
- **O**utline content summary
- **R**ehearse with notes
- **A**nimate with coloured pictures

Avoid:
Detailed lists
Numbered tables
Distracting special effects
Reading from scripts

AIMS

Decide if the purpose of your presentation is to:

Convey information   ⇒   **To tell**

Propose   ⇒   **To sell**

Motivate   ⇒   **To impel**

CONTENT

C onsider time-frame   Allow a planning to delivery ratio of 10 to 1
O rganise theme   Start with a bang
N ame all possible points   Brainstorm
T ake essential points   Keep it simple
E nter links and illustrate   Have a clear structure
N ote key points on cards   End with a bang
T est understanding   Summarise and close

TIMING

KEEP IT SHORT & SIMPLE

There is a dramatic tailing-off of information retention over time. Keep your presentations short and to the point.

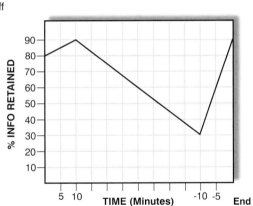

PRESENTING

PRE-DELIVERY

- Check room and facilities
- Note names and seating plan
- Map agenda and time
- Glow enthusiasm
- Deep breath
- Beam round
- Stand up
- Head up
- Speak up

PRESENTING

DELIVERY

Begin and end with a **BANG**, eg:

- Question
- Prop
- Anecdote
- Speech drama
- Action
- Surprise
- Audio-visual gimmick

- Tell 'em what you will tell 'em
- Tell 'em
- Tell 'em what you told 'em

DELIVERY

P ause often
A ccentuate
V ary tone, pitch, speed
A void um's and er's
R epeat key phrases
O pen hands in front
T ake short simple words
T alk eye to eye
I mpress with good dress and grooming

PRESENTING

DELIVERY

VHF

We recall

10% of what we read

20% of what we hear

30% of what we see

70% of what we take in through all three channels, ie: see, hear and read

V isual

H earing

F eeling

PRESENTING

AUDIENCE CONTROL

A llow time for questions
B e sensitive to their needs
C reate interest
D ecide what they should do/think at end
E licit success by commitment to progress

PRESENTING

AUDIENCE QUESTIONS

P re-empt
A llow time
L eave questions and handouts until end
S ummarise and answer straight

If faced with a difficult question:

Relay	⟹	To group
Ricochet	⟹	To expert
Reverse	⟸	To asker

PALS R 3

PRESENTING

AUDIENCE *BUZZARDS*

- Heckler ⟹ understand, find merit, move on
- Talker ⟹ wait, thank, re-focus
- Complainer ⟹ check importance, specifics
- Whisperer ⟹ freeze, beam, ask a question
- Wonderer ⟹ use analogy, example, relay
- Interrupter ⟹ enthuse, refer to agenda, note question slowly

PRESENTING

WRITTEN PROPOSALS
STRUCTURE

If you are putting forward a written proposal, use the following structure for your presentation:

1. Covering letter
2. Management summary
3. Client aims and objectives
4. Current methods and costs
5. Requirements: new conditions, needs and priorities
6. Proposed improvements
7. Implementation plan
8. Supplier's unique benefits
9. Cost-benefits and return on investment
10. Appendices

PRESENTING

WRITTEN PROPOSALS

TIPPING THE BALANCE

- Test acceptability of draft costings in advance
- Number each page
- Use graphics
- Proof-read it yourself
- Make a copy for each decision-maker
- Tailor to reader
- Submit it in person
- If competing, submit it last (**and** in time!)

WRITTEN PROPOSALS
COVERING LETTER

- Personalise to each decision-maker

- Thank them for assistance to date

- Put a deadline on the quote

- Confirm next action (**not** We await your reply)

WRITTEN PROPOSALS
VIA THIRD PARTIES

- Avoid submitting your proposal via a third party if possible
- Do their work for them: *That's my job*
- Offer to be available when they submit the proposal
- Include case studies and testimonials
- Track its route

EXHIBITIONS

Talking to prospects at an exhibition represents a sales cycle condensed into **minutes**.

- **Objective**   Qualify and sell to new prospects
- **Opportunities** New leads and visibility
- **Preparation**   Select prospects, send a mailshot and follow up by phone beforehand
- **During**   Qualify quickly

Ask them their **WANTS**

W ants   *What do you like most about …?*

A uthority   *Are you involved in specifying …?*

N eeds   *What is your company looking for?*

T imescale   *When do you expect to complete your research?*

S pending power *How much do you expect to invest?*

PRESENTING

EXHIBITIONS

Don't
- ✗ Say *Can I help you?*
- ✗ Pounce
- ✗ Line up
- ✗ Cluster
- ✗ Hover

Do
- ✔ Smile invitingly
- ✔ Keep the stand tidy
- ✔ Use enquiry forms
- ✔ Follow up quickly

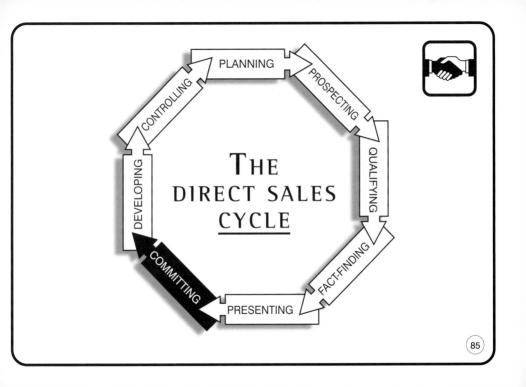

THE DIRECT SALES CYCLE

PLANNING
PROSPECTING
QUALIFYING
FACT-FINDING
PRESENTING
COMMITTING
DEVELOPING
CONTROLLING

85

COMMITTING

AGREEING BUY CRITERIA

Get potential customers to specify your Unique Service Benefits:

F ind out current criteria (if any):
   What are you looking for and why?
I ntroduce your criteria with **probing** questions:
   What if? How important is ...?
R einforce your criteria with **his/her** value on it:
   How much would that save you?

C ounterbalance your uniqueness against your competitors:
   Let's list the key points.
C ommit them to ownership:
   You've agreed these are all essential then?
C onfirm in writing:
   As you stated ...

COMMITTING

KEEPING THE INITIATIVE

- **Control** meeting agendas
- End each meeting with their **commitment to progress**
- Record commitments on **action** by **whom** by **when**
- Diary next meeting date
- **Cross-check** with phone contacts between meetings

FACE TO FACE OBJECTIONS

Most objections are **implied needs**.

- Before responding **pause** to check your body signals and think
- Reply **confidently**
- Ensure objection is resolved before moving on: *Have we covered that point to your satisfaction?*
- If benefits not yet established, **shelve it**: *Can I come back to that later?*

Price is **not** a priority if they **want** what you are selling.

Price objections mean you have not established sufficient benefits.

FACE TO FACE OBJECTIONS

- For **major** objections

  Prioritise: *How important is that?*
  Re-state as a need: *So what you're looking for is …?*
  Test close: *Is there anything else you need to consider before going ahead?*

- For **minor** objections use **feel, felt, found**:

  I understand how you **feel** *…*
  our other clients also **felt** *…*
  then they **found** *…*

COMMITTING

NEGOTIATING
PREPARATION

Before you begin negotiation, make a list of:

- Your highest and lowest acceptable **objectives**
- **Their essential** wants and needs
- **Their desirable** wants and needs
- Agreed **cost-benefits**
- **Minor** concessions you can trade

COMMITTING

NEGOTIATING
OPENING

In the meeting itself:

- Establish rapport: - confirm your commitment to their goals
  - ask permission to take notes

- Agree objectives and the follow-up process

- Summarise their agreed position to date:
  - commitment to **value** not price
  - their priorities
  - their stated buying criteria on your offer
  - benefits of operations and cost savings

COMMITTING

NEGOTIATING

MIDDLE

- State your highest objective as a minimum
- Say you have no room to manoeuvre
- Soften *No* with a logical preface
- Use the passive tense to depersonalise sensitive issues
- Use testimonials

NEGOTIATING

END

Negotiations should by now have moved to price.
When price is asked **desire** is implied.

- State price **confidently**
- Concede reluctantly in money not percentages
- Counter-balance with benefits
- Give only minor concessions
- Test close on concessions
- Make them feel like winners

COMMITTING

NEGOTIATING
LAST RESORTS TO BREAK DEADLOCKS

1. Make a time break
2. Go off the record informally
3. Suggest someone more senior replaces you
4. Refer upwards on **their** side
5. Appeal for their help

COMMITTING

CLOSING

Always
Be
Checking attitudes and reactions

Buying is emotion justified by fact.
Expressed or **implied** needs are **buying signals**.
Qualify their importance, then close. Closing means obtaining commitment **throughout**
the sales cycle.

- **Test close**: *Do you have all the information on which to make a decision?*
- **Assume close**: *When/Where will you want delivery?*
- **Alternative close**: *Shall we deliver this month or next?*
- **Justify why now**
- After asking for the order, **shut up!**

COMMITTING

ETHICS

- Provide choices without pressure
- Customers should feel they have bought, not been sold
- Avoid withholding relevant information
- Be open about limitations

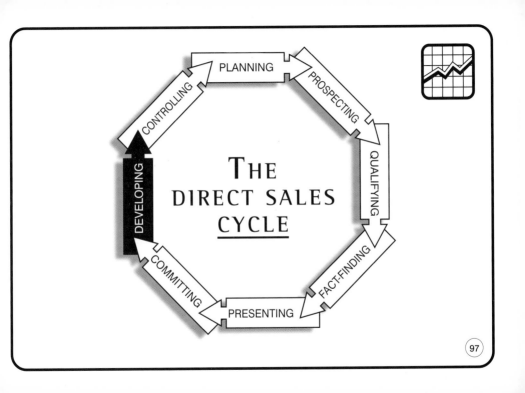

THE DIRECT SALES CYCLE

PLANNING
PROSPECTING
QUALIFYING
FACT-FINDING
PRESENTING
COMMITTING
DEVELOPING
CONTROLLING

CUSTOMER CARE

INCOMING TELEPHONE CALLS

People judge you on how well you answer their phone calls:

- Answer within four rings with a smile

- If answering an outside line, announce *Good morning/afternoon, this is XYZ company, Sam speaking. How can we help you?*

- Ask caller's name, company, contact required

- Transfer: *Thank you, transferring you now*

- If the contact is out, take telephone number and any message

CUSTOMER CARE
INCOMING TELEPHONE CALLS

Avoid

- Silences
- Waiting
- Multiple transfers
- Asking people to call back
- Saying: *He's busy / at a long lunch / don't know where / not in yet*

99

DEVELOPING

CUSTOMER CARE

- Prioritise profit potential per client:

A High short-term potential
B High long-term potential
C Low potential

- Follow the 80/20 rule (*Pareto Principle*)

80% of your business comes from 20% of your clients.

Focus on the 20%.

DEVELOPING

REFERRALS

Thank them for their business, then ask:

- *What benefits have you obtained from us?*
- *Who else could benefit likewise and why?*
- *May we say you recommend us?*

Afterwards, let your referrer know the result.
Then ask for another!

DEVELOPING

SURVEYING SATISFACTION

- Use feedback from clients to improve your service
- Set targets to assess their delight
- Use simple questionnaires by mail and telephone:
  Ask level of **satisfaction, importance and frequency** of use
- Check key quality areas:
  Delivery, packaging, manuals, installation, training, performance of service
  personnel (sales, admin, support), performance of product
- When customers stop buying, **ask why?**
  Less than 10% is because of price. Over 80% is because of poor service!

DEFUSING COMPLAINTS

BY LETTER

One complaint in **ten** reaches the suppliers
BUT
one complainer **tells ten** other prospective clients.

- Acknowledge regrets within one day
  by e-mail, fax or phone
- Give a solution date and stick to it
- Summarise issues and invite reply
- Thank them
- Follow up by phone for final OK

(103)

DEVELOPING

DEFUSING COMPLAINTS
BY PHONE

- Listen and stay calm
- Don't interrupt or pass the buck
- Ask probing questions to verify facts
- Check back your understanding
- Apologise and invite them to suggest compensation
- Agree action and timeframe
- Thank them
- Hang up phone **last**

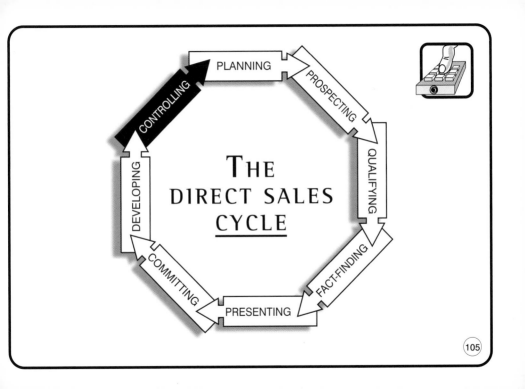

THE
DIRECT SALES
CYCLE

PLANNING

PROSPECTING

QUALIFYING

FACT-FINDING

PRESENTING

COMMITTING

DEVELOPING

CONTROLLING

(105)

FORECASTING PROBABILITY

100%	Deposit paid & installed
90%	Our paperwork signed
80%	Budget approved internally
70%	Signer(s) prefers us as supplier
60%	Recommender(s) prefers us as supplier
50%	Essential buy criteria includes our USBs
40%	Signer(s) agrees need for change
30%	Recommender(s) agrees need for change
20%	Completed fact-find & needs analysis
10%	Qualified budget, timeframe & who decides
0%	Suspect NOT prospect

KEY FORECAST DATA

- Company name and location
- Product/service to be taken
- Total value
- % probability
- Weighted value (total value x % probable)
- Top signer's name and title
- Top recommender's name and title
- Date of first visit
- Date of proposal
- Date order due
- Date of next appointment
- Known competitors

FORECASTING RED FLAGS

Each red flag reduces the forecast probability by 10%:

🚩 Top active decision-maker not met

🚩 Incomplete fact-find on **WANTS**

🚩 Changes in decision-makers/company structure

🚩 No cost-justification

🚩 Competitor's proposal was submitted before your first visit

🚩 No next appointment noted

SALES REPORTS

- Track your key results with charts showing:
  - Proposals per month
  - Calls per week
  - Forecast accuracy per client
- Share successes and challenges with the team
- Assess your own performance
- Invite support staff on joint visits

CONTROLLING

SALES REPORTS
BE A TORCH-BEARER

Q uantify in numbers not words
U se graphs
E ssential data only
S elf-analyse
T rigger action

CONTROLLING

ACTIVITY RATIOS

MAINTAIN A PIPE-LINE OF ACTIVITIES

P lot your **actual** activity numbers
I nsert activity **targets**
P lot **current** ratios
E xamine **required** ratios

Example:	CURRENT	TARGET
		(10% improvement)
Telecalls per appointment	10	9
Appointments per quotation	5	4.5
Quotations per order	3	2.7
= appointments per order	15	12
= telecalls per order	150	108

= 28% improvement!

COLLECTING PAYMENT

- The easiest time is at point of sale in person
- Qualify cheque requisition process
- Avoid conceding credit terms
- Collect deposit with order
- Mention penalty of non-payment in letter confirming order

If you experience problems:

- Don't await call-backs
- Check there have been no service problems
- Escalate to top signer
- Collect in person
- Persist

MANAGING RELATIONSHIPS

- Use case studies as signposts of your success
- Structure:
  - background scenario
  - challenges and opportunities presented
  - choices and options taken
  - outcomes and returns
- Publish with customer approval

CONTROLLING

MANAGING RELATIONSHIPS

- Be **inclusive** with all **stakeholders**
- Communicate the impact of the offer:
    - inside your business to service and support staff
    - inside your customer's supply chain
- Stakeholders include:
    - customers and suppliers
    - directors and staff
    - (and when appropriate) the community at large

MANAGING RELATIONSHIPS

- Get to know prospects as people
  - their personal likes and dislikes
  - what they **value** and why
- Disclose your own values and
  highlight shared values

115

CONTROLLING

MANAGING RELATIONSHIPS

- Create a keep-in-touch campaign
- Organise social events
- Share know-how at seminars
- Forward press articles and information on items of interest

MANAGING RELATIONSHIPS

- Keep up with competitors:
  - report special offers
  - regularly survey their **S** trengths
    W eaknesses
    O pportunities
    T hreats

- Don't criticise competitors to clients

- Do ask clients how they perceive other suppliers, especially if and why they bought from them

MANAGING RELATIONSHIPS

- Never take customer partnerships for granted
- Always look for ways to add value
- Yesterday's standard of service excellence is today's mere satisfaction and tomorrow's reason for dissatisfaction
- Benchmark against the best by using the Business Excellence Model

MANAGING RELATIONSHIPS

- Manage yourself:
  - invest in personal and professional development
  - balance life between work and home
  - seek feedback for continuous improvement

- Don't just do things right
  Do the right things right!

119

DEVELOPING NEW BUSINESS

SELF-CHECK

Score your performance on a scale of 0 = Never, 1 = Sometimes, 2 = Always.

Before making new appointments, I:

a.	have up-to-date information on strategic client issues	0	1	2
b.	use my network contacts for current grapevine news	0	1	2
c.	read their latest company report and literature	0	1	2
d.	draft my benefit statements linked to their strategy	0	1	2
e.	review their possible objections and my responses	0	1	2

When making an appointment, I:

f.	check top PA's name and title at reception	0	1	2
g.	ask for top PA's help	0	1	2
h.	check I'm not interrupting a meeting	0	1	2
i.	qualify the decision-making process and timing	0	1	2
j.	give options to facilitate **yes**	0	1	2

DEVELOPING NEW BUSINESS
SELF-CHECK

At the first meeting, I:

k.	analyse and adapt to their personal style	0 1 2
l.	emphasise my role to support their goals	0 1 2
m.	ask permission to take notes	0 1 2
n.	ask about organisation strategies	0 1 2
o.	ask about personal priorities	0 1 2

To sell my value, I:

p.	get them to expand on the *ripple effect* of issues	0 1 2
q.	ask them to estimate impact on costs and revenues	0 1 2
r.	counter-balance their cost-benefits against my costs	0 1 2
s.	build my uniqueness into their selection criteria	0 1 2
t.	reinforce with case studies and proof statements	0 1 2

THE LAST WORD

THE COST OF PRICE – THE PRICE OF VALUE

There is hardly anything in the world that some man cannot make a little worse and sell a little cheaper. People who consider price only are this man's lawful prey.

It's unwise to pay too much, but it's unwise to pay too little. When you pay too much you lose a little money, that is all. When you pay too little, you sometimes lose everything, because the thing you bought was incapable of doing the thing you bought it to do.

The common law of business balance prohibits paying a little and getting a lot. It can't be done.

If you deal with the lowest bidder, it's well to add something for the risk you run.

And if you do that, you will have enough to pay for something better.

John Ruskin

About the Author

Clive W. Bonny

Clive's early career began in financial services management. It progressed
through accounting and marketing into direct sales with British, German and
American employers. His sales career developed into major accounts and sales
management within commercial, central government and local government
sectors, consistently breaking company sales records for new business.
He was appointed General Manager in a publicly quoted American
multi-national company with profit and loss responsibility and within a two
year period he improved divisional net profits from 6.8% to 18.2% of total
revenues whilst increasing the customer base tenfold.

Clive is owner-manager of Strategic Management Partners, advising organisations on Business
Excellence and coaching individuals to improve results. Besides success in operational and board
level positions, he is a Certified Management Consultant, a Fellow of the RSA, and author of several
publications on corporate communications, career management and business ethics.

Contact

Clive can be contacted at: Strategic Management Partners, "Meadows", 18 Roedean Way, Brighton,
Sussex BN2 5RJ, England. Tel: +44 (0)1273 675924 Fax:+44 (0)1273 673960
Mobile: +44 (0)7973 799153 Website: www.consult-smp.com E-mail: CliveBonny@aol.com

"Values Sustain Value"

ORDER FORM

Your details

Name _____

Position _____

Company _____

Address _____

_____

Telephone _____

Facsimile _____

E-mail _____

VAT No. (EC companies) _____

Your Order Ref _____

Please send me:

No.
copies

The _Salesperson's_ _____ Pocketbook ☐

The _____ Pocketbook ☐

The _____ Pocketbook ☐

The _____ Pocketbook ☐

The _____ Pocketbook ☐

Order by Post

MANAGEMENT POCKETBOOKS LTD

LAUREL HOUSE, STATION APPROACH, ALRESFORD,
HAMPSHIRE SO24 9JH UK

Order by Phone, Fax or Internet

Telephone: +44 (0)1962 735573
Facsimile: +44 (0)1962 733637
E-mail: sales@pocketbook.co.uk
Web: www.pocketbook.co.uk

MANAGEMENT
POCKETBOOKS

Customers in USA should contact:
Stylus Publishing, LLC, 22883 Quicksilver Drive,
Sterling, VA 20166-2012
Telephone: 703 661 1581 or 800 232 0223
Facsimile: 703 661 1501 E-mail: styluspub@aol.com